PIANO • VOCAL • GUITAR

Selections from the Cinergi Motion Picture

EVITA

KATY GEISSERT
CIVIC CENTER LIBRARY

Lyrics by
TIM RICE

Music by
ANDREW LLOYD WEBBER

ISBN 0-7935-7845

A JOINT PUBLICATION

MCA
music publishing
A DIVISION OF UNIVERSAL ST   NC.
7777 W. BLUEMOUND RD. MILWA   3213
AND

HAL•LEON

Selections from the Cinergi Motion Picture

Contents

ON THIS NIGHT OF A THOUSAND STARS

Words by TIM RICE
Music by ANDREW LLOYD WEBBER

EVA AND MAGALDI/
EVA, BEWARE OF THE CITY

Words by TIM RICE
Music by ANDREW LLOYD WEBBER

Driving Rock

Eva: To think that a man as famous as you are could love a poor lit-tle noth-ing like me. I want to

12

Che: It seems to

14

EVA, BEWARE OF THE CITY

Moderately

say, I'll not steal you a - way!

BUENOS AIRES

Words by TIM RICE
Music by ANDREW LLOYD WEBBER

22

it's be-cause of the things __ you are. __
give your lov - er the ver - y best. __

Beau - ti - ful town,
Real ei - der down __

I love __ you.
and si - - lence.

Play 8 times

D.S. al Coda

You're a

I'D BE SURPRISINGLY GOOD FOR YOU

Words by TIM RICE
Music by ANDREW LLOYD WEBBER

ANOTHER SUITCASE IN ANOTHER HALL

Words by TIM RICE
Music by ANDREW LLOYD WEBBER

DON'T CRY FOR ME ARGENTINA

Words by TIM RICE
Music by ANDREW LLOYD WEBBER

MCA music publishing

all you have to do is look at me to know that ev-'ry word is true.

HIGH FLYING, ADORED

Words by TIM RICE
Music by ANDREW LLOYD WEBBER

Che: High fly-ing, a-dored _____ so young _____ the
High fly-ing, a-dored, _____ what hap-pens now? _____ Where do you

in-stant queen, _____ a rich beau-ti-ful thing _____ of all the
go from here? _____ For some-one on top of the world _____ the

tal-ents, _____ a cross be-tween _____ a fan-ta-sy _____ of the
view's not ex-act-ly clear, _____ a shame you did it all

RAINBOW HIGH

Words by TIM RICE
Music by ANDREW LLOYD WEBBER

Agitated

Eva: There a-gain I've more to do than sim-ply get the

mes - sage through, I have-n't start - ed! Let's

get this show on the road, let's make it ob-vi-ous Pe-ron is off and roll - ing

MCA music publishing

Faster

go; we'll put on a show!

Look out might-y Eu-rope! Be-cause you ought-ta know

what-cha gon-na get in me:__ just a lit-tle touch of, just__ a lit-

-tle touch of Ar - gen - ti - na's brand of star qual-i-ty!__

AND THE MONEY KEPT ROLLING IN (AND OUT)

Words by TIM RICE
Music by ANDREW LLOYD WEBBER

WALTZ FOR EVA AND CHE

Words by TIM RICE
Music by ANDREW LLOYD WEBBER

Bright Waltz

Che: Tell me be-fore I waltz out of your life, be-fore turn-ing my

back on the past. _____ For - give my im - per - tin-ent be -

hav - iour, but how long do you think this pan - to-mime can

68

SHE IS A DIAMOND

Words by TIM RICE
Music by ANDREW LLOYD WEBBER

YOU MUST LOVE ME

Words by TIM RICE
Music by ANDREW LLOYD WEBBER

MCA music publishing

Additional Lyrics

Verse 2: *(Instrumental 8 bars)*
Why are you at my side?
How can I be any use to you now?
Give me a chance and I'll let you see how
Nothing has changed.
Deep in my heart I'm concealing
Things that I'm longing to say,
Scared to confess what I'm feeling
Frightened you'll slip away,
You must love me.

TOP LINE

Additional Lyrics

Verse 2: (Instrumental 8 bars)
Why are you at my side?
How can I be any use to you now?
Give me a chance and I'll let you see how
Nothing has changed.
Deep in my heart I'm concealing
Things that I'm longing to say,
Scared to confess what I'm feeling
Frightened you'll slip away,
You must love me.